CHANDLER PARK BRANCH
DATE DUE

The African-American Guide to Better English

An African-American Survival Manual for
Speaking and Writing

By

Garrard O. McClendon

First Edition

HAMPTON ACADEMIC PRESS

POSITIVE PEOPLE PUBLISHING, Inc.
Chicago　　Hampton　　Culver

DEDICATION

This book was written with inspiration from my grandfathers.

William Anderson McClendon passed away many years before my birth but through my father he handed down his legacy of knowledge, pride, and the ability to strive for excellence.

Theodore Jones stressed the importance of education and communication. He not only stressed the importance of speaking correctly; he used correct English at all times. Fourteen days before his death, he told me to write a book.

ACKNOWLEDGEMENTS

I thank God because without Him I can do nothing.

Publisher
Thanks to Hampton Academic Press for believing in an
unknown, unpublished writer.

Family
Ma and Daddy : my best teachers
Granny and Gramps: always giving
Duane: advice, kindness, and encouragement
Ted: the importance of the means of production
Bill and Sylvia McClendon: archives, love, and family trees
Napoleon McClendon: always encouraging graduate school
Irene Hayes-McClendon: the spirit to venture & try new cities

Scholarly Advice
Alexis DeVeaux, Thomas Campbell, Warren Rosenberg, Tobey Herzog,
Barb Livdahl, Frederick Brigham, Edward L. Brock, Cassel White,
Paul Hamer, James Albers, Mary Frances England, Nandini Battacharya,
and Renu Juneja

Guidance
Horace Turner, Rob Johnson and the Malcolm X Institute, Khari Modeira
(Harvey Johnson), H. Khalif Khalifa, Jawanza Kunjufu, Kendryck Allen,
Ben Brown, Charles Burns, Paul Warner, Danny Dillard, Cheikh Sene, Akare
(John Aden), Michael Robinson, Jeff Cusic and all my gifted friends from
Wabash College and Valparaiso University

The African-American Guide to Better English

An African-American Survival Manual for
Speaking and Writing

By

Garrard O. McClendon

First Edition

The African-American Guide to Better English
was written by Garrard O. McClendon.

A HAMPTON ACADEMIC PRESS BOOK
distributed and published for
POSITIVE PEOPLE, INC.
P.O. Box 4
Culver, IN 46511
312-839-3442
219-751-0000

Library of Congress Cataloging-in-Publication Data
CIP CATALOG CARD NUMBER 93-80308

McClendon, Garrard O., 1966-
The African-American Guide to Better English

    I.   English language--Rhetoric
    II.   Dialects/Colloquialisms
    III.   African-American Studies
    IV.   Linguistics--Black Vernacular English

ISBN#   0-9639329-0-X

SPECIAL THANKS

A mark of special appreciation to **Michell Denene Carter**
for being supportive throughout the writing process and for
providing hope in uncomfortable
situations. Your prayers and actions have benefitted me
greatly and I thank God for you, your
belief, and your encouraging spirit.

So one of our greatest desires is to try to broaden the scope and reading habits of most of our people, who need their scope and reading habits broadened today.

Malcolm X, January 24, 1965

...when you read, you may understand my knowledge in the mystery of Christ.

Ephesians 3:4

Train a child up in the way he should go: and when he is old, he will not depart from it.

Proverbs 22:6

The very time I thought I was lost,
My dungeon shook and my chains fell off.

African-American Proverb

iv.

PREFACE

This book was in no way created to try to insult or diminish the speech patterns of African-Americans. This book's purpose is to inform the Black community of the devices used against it to perpetuate the misuse and disuse of language.

Slang, jargon, and colloquialisms make the speech of African-Americans colorful. However as W.E.B. DuBois warns us in his book, *The Souls of Black Folk*, African-Americans must possess a duality in the United States. My stance on this is that African-Americans must have a duality consisting of Black Vernacular English (the language of the neighborhood) and standard American English (the language of power and finance). Opportunities can be discarded without using standard American English.

While it is clear that nobody completely speaks standard American English in the United States (including television news anchors, politicians, and teachers), African-Americans should take extra care and study this book to avoid many of the pitfalls in language that may act as stumbling blocks in more formal conversation and writing.

Job interviews, classroom discussions, and basic conversation with those outside of the Black community can become disastrous if standard American English isn't used appropriately when needed.

In this book you will see several examples of words and expressions misused by many African-Americans in formal environments. Although all of these examples aren't restricted to just the African-American community, most prove to be prevalent.

This book can be used by anyone for the improvement of speech, grammar, or personal reference, but its target is the African-American.

Garrard McClendon

CONTENTS

The African-American Guide to Better English

Chapter 1

A Time and a Place for Black English

If you want to commit job interview suicide, try wearing jeans and sandals to an interview. Though this may sound like a silly example, it's meant to be taken seriously. So stands the case of language usage outside of standard American English. Unfamiliar slang, Black Vernacular English, or foul language can hinder a candidate's chances of getting a job if used during an interview. You may also lose the person's interest or respect. You must try your best to adhere to the rules of Standard American English, because being understood is the reason why we communicate.

If there are ten applicants for a job and eight are eliminated in the application and resume process, it's a strong possibility that the eight eliminated didn't have the qualifications or they submitted sub-par applications and resumes.

If you are one of the two chosen to have an interview, you must now pass stage two. Finding a candidate who will represent the company best will be the interview's purpose at this point and then an employee will be selected. In your interview, clothing, hair style, accessories, fragrance (or no fragrance), facial expression, knowledge of the company and most important, diction, must be flawless.

Why is diction (the way one enunciates and uses speech) important? Your potential employer is looking at whom she would like to have as a representative of the company. A good command of the language wins every time. Whether you're applying at a computer company or fast food restaurant, put your best foot forward. Applicants always outnumber jobs available, so you should practice speaking skills alone or with a friend or family member. In metropolitan areas, there are also learning and speaking centers that specialize in the improvement of speaking skills. Employed at such centers are speech pathologists, therapists, phonologists and coaches. Their function is to aid the deficient speaker in the weaker area diagnosed, including word pronunciation, hearing, tongue and lip positioning, diction, and timing.

When in doubt about language, ask a question. This will save embarrassment. Pajamas are comfortable at home, but that doesn't give everyone the liberty to wear them everywhere. In formal arenas use standard American English. Among friends, feel free to talk as you wish.

In the next chapter we will discuss some of the common mistakes made by African-Americans. Studying the glossary should help you with your speaking and writing skills.

Forbidden Words, Definitions, Phrases, and Pronunciations

Ask

The definition of ask is "to call for an answer to or about." Many pronounce this word with the "s" and "k" inverted; thus, pronouncing the word incorrectly as "aks" or "ax." The correct pronunciation places the "s" before the "k" as in the words "task," "bask," "flask," and "mask." The Tindel translation of the King James Version of the Bible spells this as: axeth. This is outdated, therefore we should use today's spelling and pronunciation as listed above.

Ain't

Ain't is a *verb form*, colloquial contraction meaning *aren't* or expressing a negative (am not, is not). This should never be used in formal speech or writing. *Ain't* is often used in conversation and is rarely written, but during a job interview you shouldn't make use of the word.

Nonstandard: This *ain't* the way to Chicago.

Standard: This *is not* the way to Chicago.

Ambulance (am-byoo-lens)

Many pronounce this word in the way they have heard it said around the house. Some pronounce it "am'bah'lans" others "ammuh'lams." Both ways are incorrect and the person who is unsure should correct the pronunciation before using in an interview. It would be a shame to apply for a job at the hospital and not be able to pronounce ambulance correctly.

Aggravate/Irritate

Aggravate means "to make worse." You cannot aggravate something that isn't already bad. *Irritate* means "to annoy."

Amen (ay-men) (ah-men)

In no way am I going to try to attempt to change the way Black people say this word, especially in church during a good sermon. The word should be pronounced (ay-men) or (ah-men) with the second syllable as men, *not* "man." Commonly mispronounced "a-man" but incorrect nevertheless.

Aluminum (al-loo-min-num)

There is only one "n" in aluminum. Be sure not to put 2 "n's" around the "m." Some say the word "aluminin" or "alunimun." You *can* really sound illiterate if you don't pronounce this with care. If you can't say it, practice it alone.

a.m. (ante meridiem)

Means *before noon*. Saying something twice can be an honest mistake but try to avoid this "redundant devil." If you say "5 in the morning," this is acceptable. But if you say "5 *a.m.* in the morning," this is redundant because *a.m.* already implies morning (see definition above). What you say in public gives an impression. Be careful with language usage.

Alphabet (al-fuh-bet)   Album (al-bum)
Alcohol (al-co-hall)   Algebra (al-juh-bruh)

These can be very annoying words because many say the words without pronouncing the "l." Enunciate each letter and each syllable.

Abominable (uh-bom-eh-nuh-bel)

Means *detestable*. Nearly everyone has problems with words like this. Look at it and sound it out (slowly).

Aunt (awnt)

Do not say "auntie," "awntie," or "ant" in a formal situation. Feel free to use these at home or with friends. I've used all 3 and all 3 are informal. The correct pronunciation is provided. In formal speech, think before you say "awntie."

Atlanta/Atlantic/Pacific

The "t's" must be pronounced (At-lan-tah), not (Allana). The second sounds like a girl's name. Also say (At-lan-tik) as in the ocean. Do not put the "s" on Pacific Ocean making it *Spacific* Ocean. Don't laugh; I've heard this many times. It's (Puh-si-fik).

Attempt

Tricky to pronounce for some, but not for others. Always pronounce the last "t" in the word; do not cut it off by saying "attemp."

Athlete

Do not add the third syllable to this word. It has 2 syllables and is pronounced "ath-leet," not "ath-a-leet."

Authentic

Pronounce the last "t" in authentic also. Do not cut by saying "awthennick." Cutting the letters off of words can covertly suggest that you're lazy and careless in your speech.

Answer

Do not cut off "r" at the end of the word *answer*. Some say "ansuh" and this can be difficult to understand depending on who is listening. Also make sure that you do *not* pronounce the "w" in the word.

Among/Between

Incorrect: Tyrone couldn't choose between the three desserts.

Correct: Tyrone couldn't choose from the three desserts.

Incorrect: Julia saw me *among* one lady.

Correct: Julia saw me *among* three ladies.

Generally, when more than two things or more than two people are involved, *among* is used. *Between* is used when referring to two objects or things.

Anxious (aink-shus)

Please do not mistake anxious for eager or the inverse. Eager means "having keen desire or longing" whereas anxious means "full of anxiety, worried." Correct examples:

I was *eager* to see my oldest brother.

I was *anxious* to see my bad report card.

Bad

Bad meaning bad or *bad* meaning good? This word can be tricky in many conversations that require accuracy. *Bad* meaning "good" is slang and should be avoided if around unfamiliar people.

Be

The verb *be* has always been misused in the Black community. Black people have destroyed the *be* verb formally, but when you're with your peer group, feel free to use it if you choose. Sentences with the verb *be* used incorrectly look like this one:

We be going to the store after we get paid.

These are correct:

We are going to the store after we get paid.
We will go to the store after we get paid.

I won't get into it any further but care should be taken before using this word. The *be* verbs are *be, am, is, are, was, were, been, being.*

Band-Aid/bandage

Band-Aid is a company that makes bandages. Don't confuse the brand name with the product. A bandage is something used to protect an open sore or cut. **See Vaseline and Kleenex.**

Bathroom/Birthday

Pronounce the "th" in both words. Many people put an "f" sound in there somewhere making the words sound like this: baf-room and birf-day. No! Many times this pronunciation is due to association and what is heard in the home and in the peer group.

Band

Articulate the "d" at the end of the word. It's easy to cut it off it in a sentence. *Sand* is similar.

Biblical Spelling and Pronunciation

The Holy Bible has many words that are very difficult to say and spell. Many Bible interpretations (editions) will have pronunciation keys, so it is best to use them. Sounding out words is best on the first try, but if you aren't sure, ask or check the keys. Just as you would not want your name mispronounced, neither should you mispronounce anyone else's name (be it in the Bible or in an everyday situation). Many of our ministers have trouble with some Bible words and this sends out a message subject to many interpretations. Study to show thyself approved.

Brought/Bought

The verbs *bring* and *buy* are often confused. You must make it a point to think before speaking when using these words. The past tense for *bring* is *brought*. The past tense for *buy* is *bought*. Below are some examples of incorrect and correct usage.

Incorrect: I *brought* the bicycle from the salesperson for one hundred dollars.
               I *bought* this game from home.

Correct: I *bought* the bicycle from the salesperson for one hundred dollars.
               I *brought* this game from home.

Breath

Here's another word that many children mispronounce. The "th" at the end of the word is pronounced by placing the tongue against the upper front teeth before articulation. This ensures the "th" sound. Some people may pronounce this as "bref," but "bref" requires the upper front teeth on the bottom lip. This action shouldn't occur while saying this word.

Buffet

Buffet has a silent "t" at the end. It is pronounced (buff-fay) not (buff-fet). This pertains to meals or food bought in a line without service. *Buffet* has a french origin and a french pronunciation (silent "t").

Break/Brake

Watch the confusion of these words. Two different meanings and spellings occur here.

Break means to separate into pieces under blow or strain; shatter or disconnect to make inoperative.

Brake means a device for stopping motion of wheel or vehicle.

Busted/Bursted/Bust

All are incorrect. The correct form that should be used is the word *burst. Burst* should be used in the past, present , future, and past participle forms.

Yesterday the balloon burst.
Today the balloon burst.
Tomorrow the balloon will burst.

Business

Business is **not** pronounced with a "d" sound in it anywhere. Those of you who say "bid-ness" know who you are.

Beach/Beech

If you misspell one of these words, you will confuse your reader. A *beach* is a pebbly or sandy shore, but a *beech* is a forest tree with smooth bark and glossy leaves.

Calendar/Calender

Calendar with an "a" at the end is what we use for dates (month, year). *Calender* with an "e" at the end is a machine for rolling cloth or paper. They are pronounced identically so watch your spelling. This is a somewhat excusable mistake.

Can I, May I

Can denotes ability. *May* represents permission. Don't confuse the two. Examples of proper use are found below:

Can I jump higher than Larry Johnson?
May I have some cookies and cake?

Certificate (ser-ti-fi-kit)

I've heard this word said in many ways from *susificate* to *certifisus*. Actually it is a simple four syllable word but saying it slowly is probably the best way to saying it correctly.

Colloquialism (everyday speech)

Colloquialisms, slang words or phrases, and jargon should be avoided in formal situations. This can easily offend people or exclude them from conversation. However, if the situation calls for a looser structure, feel free to interject colloquialisms. Once you become more familiar with an individual or group, some parts of everyday speech are allowed.

Confide/Confine

These words have different meanings. To express that you've confided in someone is one thing, but to confined someone is another. *Confide* is to tell a secret or to entrust. *Confine* is to keep or restrict.

Cope

An intransitive verb used with the word *with*. In formal writing, one doesn't "cope," but one "copes with" something or somebody.

Informal: *Gladys coped.*

Formal: *Gladys coped with the terrible situation.*

Crib/House

If you ever make this mistake in a formal situation, you had better laugh it off quickly, or say the word *house* as quickly as you can. Generally this term is a regional one, but concentrate before you speak and say the word *house* instead of *crib*. I use the word *crib* because it feels more comfortable when I'm around my friends. But in a changing environment, use the predominant language of the environs. *Crib* also has some negative historic connotations that have been studied by sociologists. Some believe that the Black man uses this word to express his diminutive status in terms of ownership (Blacks being able to own *cribs*, but not big houses). Some also think that this is linked with many Blacks referring to their friends as "babies" (as in, "what's up, baby?") and referring to white men as "the man." Though I have some reservations about these origins, one could possibly find some value or feasibility in this theory.

Dial (dy-el)

With this word, pronunciation is very important because someone may interpret your saying of *dial* as something else. Don't cut the "l" off of this word. The key to pronunciation and sounding literate is simply the articulation of every syllable and every letter that should be pronounced. I've heard this pronounced *"die," "di'uh," and "doll."* Speak clearly because first impressions are important.

Dis

Dis, as a colloquial expression means to discount or disrespect. One can make this word invention sound formal depending on how the word is delivered but avoiding this word would be advisable. Some pronounce "this" as "dis" too. You may get "dissed" in a job interview if you use "dis."

Dobermann pinscher

It's not "Domomann" or "Dobo mann" pinscher. The correct way to say it is (Do-ber-mann). Children in the neighborhood destroy this pronunciation. Let's teach them the right way to say it. *Pinscher* is pronounced (pin-chur).

Door

Pronounce "r" at the end. Do not say "doe."

Drawers

Pronounced (draw-ers), this is another word for underwear and colloquially this is said in the Black community as "draws" for effect. Please say this correctly in mixed public or someone else may not have any idea what you're talking about.

Double Negatives

Two negatives in a sentence should not be used together. We as a people, love double negatives so be careful in formal speech. Below are definite *no no's.*

I ain't got none.
We don't have no money.

You can easily correct these by saying or writing:

I don't have any. I have none.
We don't have any money. We have no money.

Drowned (drown'd)

Similar to *skinned,* drowned is not pronounced with the extra "ded" on the end: drowned (drown'd), not drownded (drownded). **See *skinned.***

Enthusiasm

Be very careful not to say *enthused* because the word it comes from is *enthusiasm.* In everyday talk, people will say *enthuse* but this is not standard American English. Say the entire word *enthusiasm* in order to avoid confusion.

Informal: I was *enthused* when I heard the verdict of the court trial.
Formal: I was *enthusiastic* when I heard the verdict of the court trial.

Experience (*Eks-peer-ee-ens*)

Do not cut off any syllables or letters in this word. Some mispronounce this one (ex-spince).

Expect/Suspect

Expect and *suspect* have different definitions. *Expect* is the assumption of a future event. *Suspect* means to be inclined to think (of,that); mentally accuse of; as a noun it means a person who has been accused, or has potential of being accused. Below are two examples used correctly.

I *expect* Michell to be here at 8:00 P.M.
I *suspect* that Jeffrey has stolen my train set.

Et cetera (et-set-er-uh)

Etc. or *et cetera* means "and other things." Please delete it from your written works. It is often over used in speech as well. I often misuse this one in the classroom while lecturing.

Fix

Strunk and White's book, *The Elements of Style*, shows how this term can be abused in a few ways. Some Blacks often add to the complexity of this word by saying the phrase, "fixin' to" or "finnah." This means "to get ready..." and falls in line with the colloquial meaning for the word, *to arrange, to prepare,* or *to mend,* but the word is from *figere* which means "to make firm," or "to place definitely." An example of this usage would be:

> *I'm fixin' to go to the store.*

You should say:

> *I'm preparing (or getting ready) to go to the store.*

Be very careful with words and phrases you've grown up with around your house and neighborhood. These words could be interpreted as inarticulate and could cause a negative response at an interview.

February

February has 2 (two) "r's" so pronounce them both. Do not say *Febuary.* The second syllable, *bru,* is pronounced like it is spelled. Sounded out, the word would be pronounced: Feh-brew-air-eee.

Feh (eh sound as in leg), Brew (u sound as in you), Air (as in Air Jordan), E (as in squeak).

Female Dog

The "B" Word is overused by many uncouth African-Americans who use word to offend women. Also used by men or women when referring to a man who is considered to be "soft," effeminate, or weak;

He's acting like a b....because he won't lift the barbell.

Having many different dynamic uses, it can also be used to describe someone with a strong will or lack of tolerance.

The b....y attitude of the CEO wouldn't make allowances for our absences.

Please avoid the word at all costs when referring to people. Use only when discussing female dogs, wolves, foxes, or otters. *derog.* sly or spiteful person. **Also see section on vulgar words.**

Fellows

Pronounced like *bellow* or *mellow*. This word isn't exclusive to the Black community but in a formal situation say *fellows*, not *fellas*.

Film

Many of us say *fim*, while forgetting the *"l"* in the middle of the word. I have also heard this word pronounced *fil-um*. The words, *pattern* and *film*, have consonants at the end. Do not place vowel sounds between these consonants. **See *pattern*.**

Found

There is no "t" sound at the end of this word. Do not say *fount*. A "d" sound is present at the end of *found*.

Freeze/Squeeze

These two words can be very confusing in the past tense and past participle. Use accordingly.

Present	Past	Past Participle
freeze	froze	frozen
squeeze	squeezed	squeezed

Frustrated

Do not place the letter "l" in the word *frustrated*. It does not have an "l" and its first syllable is "frus," not "flus." The correction may be frustrating but with practice, it will eventually work itself out.

Gwine

This is another way of saying the word *going*. *Gwine* is seen in slave narratives, late19th and early 20th century novels, and it is heard in speech by those in the south who adhere to Black Vernacular and Southern dialect from earlier years. Delete from formal speech.

I's *gwine* to the store.

This sentence should be replaced with this statement.

I am *going* to the store.

Government

Not only exclusive to the Black community but a word that should be articulated properly. One tendency is to become lazy and just say *guv'ment* or *guvva'ment*.

Grasshopper/Firefly/Beetle

Above you will see the correct words for our friends in the insect world. Sometimes *grasshopper* is inverted and pronounced *hoppergrass*. As a child I used to always use the colloquial form for *firefly* which is *lightning bug*. I also used the expression *pinching bug* instead of *beetle*. These aren't that crucial in everyday speech, but try to adapt when possible.

Gray Areas

There are some areas in language that are gray. Gray meaning that some situations need to be formal all the time, and others needing formality sometimes. You will have to judge this by your interaction with others, formally and informally. A gray area would allow a term of jargon or slang to be used informally if both are aware of the term and both are comfortable with the term. There are certain common phrases that are acceptable because the majority of the speaking society is familiar with the phrase. Keep speech simple for clarity.

Good/Well

These are two, tricky words. Many still have problems with these words but if you follow the rule, you will not stumble. Here's the rule: *Good* is an adjective and often follows a linking verb.

The silk scarf feels *good.*

Well is an adverb and often follows an action verb. However, when *well* means "in good health," "attractive," or "satisfactory," it is used as an adjective.

I work *well* in the morning. [adverb]
Christina doesn't feel *well.* [adjective --- "in good health"]

Hanged/Hung

People are hanged; objects are hung. Hence, you should **not** say: *The penalty for the criminal was for him to be hung.* Since people are *hanged,* you must say: *The penalty for the criminal was for him to be hanged.* If you are referring to a picture on the wall, you should say: *I hung the picture on the wall.*

Homonyms

Homonyms are words that look alike or sound alike but have different meanings. Be sure not to confuse words because of their homonymic structure. Two examples are *some/sum* and *sun/son.* Though the words in each sound alike, their definitions differ. Be careful not to misspell in formal writing.

Hisself

This is non-standard for *himself.*

Humiliate/Humility

Humiliate means to harm the dignity or self-respect of someone. *Humility* means a humble attitude of mind. Do not confuse the two.

Hundred (hun'drid)

Many people make the mistake of saying the following:

Give me a *hunnerd* dollars.

Give me a *hunna* dollars.

hunnid

You must be careful of pronunciation. It is a two syllable word (hun'drid).

Ignorant (ig-nuh-rent) (ig-nor-ent)

A three syllable word, not a two syllable. Do not pronounce (ig-nent) or (ig-na-nent) because you will look ignorant doing this.

Iron

Pronounced (i'urn). Oh haven't you heard many of us pronounce this word as a one syllable word (arn)? It does have two syllables so say them both, (eye-urn) or (eye-ern).

Irregardless/Regardless

Regardless means without regard or consideration, therefore, *irregardless* is a double negative. *Regardless* is saying without regard; *irregardless* is saying without no regard, hence the double negative. Make it easy on yourself and say *regardless*. The word *irregardless* is not standard and is erroneous.

Jewelry

Jewelry is not pronounced "jury" or "jew-ry." The "l" is pronounced. Try saying it slow with the following phonetic pronunciations (jew-well-ree), (jewel-ry).

Kindergarten

The mispronunciation of *kindergarten* is painful to my ears. I've seen many children, at 5 and 6 years old, who cannot pronounce the grade in school that they are currently attending. How many parents and children have constantly said "kenny-garden" or "kinna-garden"? Speech starts at a young age and we must take care in teaching the child. How can we expect our children to be articulate if we don't reinforce spelling, diction, and what is appropriate in the home?

Kleenex

Kleenex is a product name for a facial tissue. All facial tissues aren't Kleenex, therefore be specific and not vague with this usage. Other facial tissue companies have names such as the Puffs facial tissue company. **See Vaseline and Band-Aid.**

Lackadaisical

Unenthusiastic. This word's first syllable is pronounced *lack*, not *lax* or lacks. Though its somewhat related to the word *lax* and *laxity* it is not pronounced like them. *Lack-eh-day-zi-kel* isn't a hard word to pronounce, though many have heard it incorrectly and perpetuate the mispronunciation.

Learn/Teach

Learn is something a student does. *Teach* is what the instructor does. Therefore one should not say the following:

> *Learn me how to play the guitar.*

One should say:

> *Teach me how to play the guitar.*

Leave/Let

Leave and *let* are misused in speech.

Incorrect:	*Leave* the children play in the park.
Correct:	*Let* the children play in the park.
Incorrect:	*Let* him alone.
Correct:	*Leave* him alone.

Live/Live

There are two pronunciations. One has a short "i" sound as in (liv) and the other a long "i" as in (lyv).

Loan/Lend/Borrow

Loan is a noun. When using verb tense, one should use the word *lend.* When using nouns as verbs, you can confuse the listener. Sentences like the following would not be appropriate.

Car me around the city.
Loan me a dollar.

But the following sentences, with the verb replacement would be fine.

Drive me around the city.
Lend me twenty dollars.

Do you see the major difference? You should, but if not, study the rule and examples. *Borrow me a dollar.*

This should be:
Lend me a dollar.

Looked (look-t)

Looked is a word which is similar to *skinned* in its pronunciation. Be careful not to say (look-tid). Yes indeed. You have definitely heard Black children and adults say "looktid" as in, "That girl look-tid good!"

Minneapolis and Indianapolis

Tricky, tricky, tricky! Sound out the letters and syllables in these two big cities and you should be able to eliminate your pronunciation problem. Never say the words too fast. *Connecticut* and Massachusetts are two other tough ones.

Modern

Modern has two syllables, not three. Do not say "mo-der-in." **See *pattern and southern*.**

Names of Writers and Artists

I have an anecdote pertaining to this category. I was in a bookstore one day and a young lady tried to impress me with her words. I walked to the counter with a stack of books to purchase and we started talking about writers. First we mentioned some contemporaries and then we ventured into history. Out of the blue, she mentions Albert Camus. This was fine but she didn't have a clue on how to say the author's name correctly. Communication served its purpose because I knew who she was talking about, but her pronunciation was a disaster. The "s" that ends Albert Camus is a silent one and she pronounced that "s" over and over. By this time, I was driven right up the wall. She later mentioned another writer, Dostoevsky, and needless to say, I was "too through." After I politely corrected her, we still continued our discussion. It was a tragedy to see this 34 year old Black woman mispronounce these words, but it proves that we can all learn something everyday, despite age or education. I've made mistakes like this too and I'm not saying I'm perfect. Research is important for all of us because we all have deficiencies (including the author).

Nan

Nan is an expression that means "none." Often used in conjunction with "one," this word should not be used at all in formal situations.

Informal: I don't want *nan* one of them men because they ain't makin' no money.

This is a better way to say the above thought.

Formal: I don't want any of those men because they don't have any money.

Nauseous/Nauseated

The first means "sickening to contemplate"; the second means "sick to the stomach." Do not, therefore, say "I feel nauseous," unless you are sure you have that effect on others (Strunk & White -- The Elements of Style).

Nigger

Nobody in the world should use this term. In some parts of England, the word is punishable. It's too bad it's not punishable in the United States. The term is a derogatory term referring to Africans. In Anthony T. Browder's book, *From the Browder Files*, Browder tells us that it derives from *necro*, which means dead. Negro means black and comes from the Spanish definition which isn't so bad. The reality is that the word *nigger* was created to degrade and to subhumanize Africans in the middle passage and in slavery. The sad end to the story is that we as a people use it on each other to degrade. Release this burden from your vocabulary. *Necro*, to *Negro*, to *nigger*. What an evolution? And you ask, what's in a name? Plenty!

Numbers

Enunciate numbers with crisp consonants. It is easy to get into the habit of saying, *foe* instead of *four*, *fi* instead of *five*, and *naan* instead of *nine*. Functional pronunciation and literacy is important in situations outside of our community.

Oil

Oil has regional pronunciations. The great midwestern dialect has this pronunciation (oy-el). It is pronounced (all) and (erl) in some regions but for formal situations, safety would have us use the (oy-el) pronunciation.

Pattern (pat'ern) (pat'urn)

Pattern is pronounced (pat'urn); it is **not** pronounced (pat'er'in). It doesn't end with a third syllable (in). It's two syllables.

Picture

Pronounced (pick-chur), not pitcher.

Plurals

Be on the look out for words that do **not** simply take an "s" at the end to make plural. Words like *leaf, shelf, and half,* change form when in the plural. *Leaf* becomes *leaves, shelf* becomes *shelves,* and *half* becomes *halves.* Be careful with the plural of men/women. Never say mens, unless it's possessive (men's).

Polish/polish

This word is pronounced two ways. Actually there are two different words here. One means to clean or buff something and to make smooth and glossy by rubbing. Its pronunciation is (pah-lish) with a short vowel sound. The other is Polish as in a citizen of Poland. Its pronounced (poh-lish) with a long "o."

Poor

Pronounced (poor) not po'.

Psychology/Psalm/Psoriases

Though they all start with a "p" they do not have the "p" sound. The "p" is silent.

Quarter

Ahhh, I've heard this pronounced "quota" but it's (qwar-ter).

Racial and Sexual Slurs

Please avoid these in the words of Malcolm X, "by any means necessary." Racial and sexual slurs do not help anyone and they are only a vehicle to put down others, making them appear to be inferior or subhuman. Don't use these in private or public because it blatantly (overtly) shows that you are a racist or sexist. Telling an ethnic joke displays a high level of intolerance, ignorance, and inequality. Words are powerful, so choose them wisely.

Read

This word has two different pronunciations. The present tense pronunciation is (reed), but the past tense pronunciation is (red) like the color.

I *read (reed)* many books in my spare time.
I have *read (red)* many books over the last summer.

Relevant (rel-uh-vent)

Do not switch the "v" and "l" or you'll have the word *revelent. Rel* is the first syllable (not *rev*).

Respectively and Respectfully

Don't use interchangeably. *Respectively* deals with the order of something, *respectfully* deals with respect. See correct uses below.

I kissed my mother and my girlfriend, respectively. (order)

Respectfully, I bowed for the audience. (respect)

Right Fast

An overused expression in the Black community that is often said when referring to something happening quickly. Actually the word "momentarily" or the expression "in a moment" should be used. In some cases, the word *quickly* could be used to replace *right fast*.

> Informal: Hold on *right fast*; I have a phone
> call on the other line.
> Wait *right fast*, I'm getting her address.

> Formal: Hold *momentarily*; I have a call on the other line.
> Wait for a *moment*; I'm getting her address.

Try to eliminate *right fast* from your speaking vocabulary because if you continue to use it in informal situations, you may use it in formal ones.

Sandwich

Please pronounce the "d," "w," and the "ch" in this word. It is very easy to say "sam-mich," "san-wich," and "san-mich" instead of *sand-wich*. Laziness can make you sound inarticulate.

Skinned (skinned)

Not *skinded*. There is one "d" in this word. Say *skinned* not *skin-ded*. I still slip on this one from time to time. Be careful. **Also see *looked*.**

Southern

Southern has two syllables (su-thern), not three as in "su-ther-in." The words *modern* and *pattern* also have two syllables. Do not add the extra "in" syllable.

Statistic

This word is a tongue twister for many people. Saying it slowly is the key. Break it down into three syllables (sta-tis-tick). Practicing will do wonders.

Subtle

In class, I've heard this pronounced "sub-tl." The "b" in *subtle* is so subtle you can't hear it. It is silent, therefore cut it out of pronunciation. *Subtle* means hard to detect or to describe.

Suburb

Suburb has one "r" in it. I've heard this pronounced "sur-burb" and "sub-ub." Be very careful with this word.

Supposedly

Don't place the letter "b" in this one. It is (sup-po-sed-ly), not (sup-po-sub-ly).

Subject/Verb Agreement

Make sure that your subject always agrees with your verb. If you have a plural subject, your verb must match it or your sentence will sound awkward.

Do not make these common mistakes.

The boys and girls plays dominoes
The boy play the piano.

These are the correct sentences.

The boys and girls play dominoes each day.
The boy plays the piano.

Try and...

This expression is not restricted to African-Americans but often those in the Black community abuse this to no end.

Try and make some money. Try and see if he can go .
See if you can try and buy those new Kani jeans.

The action here is "trying to do" something not (try and). Check yourself on this one and practice alone with repetition. *Try to, try to, try to...*

The correct usage would be: *Try to make some money.*

Their/There/They're

These three are serious spelling demons. Because they sound alike, you must be careful in your proofreading, not to miss these. *Their* signifies possession; *there* denotes location; and *they're* is the contraction for "they are."

Than/Then

Than is a statement of comparison. *Then* means "at that time," "after," "next." Please spell correctly depending upon use.

I am taller *than* you.
Since *then,* two motorists have been killed at that location.

To/Too/Two

All of these words sound alike but they have different definitions and spellings. Remember the homonyms we saw earlier? *To* introduces a noun or expresses what is reached; *too* means "to a greater extent than desirable or permissible;" *two* is a number (2).

Through

Pronounced: (throo). The "r" is important. How many times have we heard or said, "I'm thoo' cutting the grass."

Use to could

Avoid this expression and just say, "was once able," or "used to be able." This is a common expression among children.

Incorrect: *I used to could beat you running.*
Correct: *I used to be able to beat you running.*
          I was once able to run faster than you.

Unique

We know how to seriously use this word out of context. Often we are taught to say this word and use it out of its definition. The word cannot be comparative or superlative. It simply means "without like or equal," which means that degrees of uniqueness are impossible. Incorrect use is seen below:

His Cherokee Blazer is more unique than yours.

To clean up the above sentence, we should take out the degree, as stated in the definition, and simply state that the Blazer is *unique.*

His Cherokee Blazer is unique; yours is like the others.

This keeps the sentence simple also, and does not allow you to get into a verbal war over whose vehicle is *more unique.* It is simply, *unique.*

<u>Variations in Pronunciation</u>

Words that make the English language complicated are vowel sounds with "strange, silent" letters in them. Here are a few examples.

Through, bough, though, rough, and bought all have different pronunciations. But if you'll notice, their endings are alike. They all have the letters "ough" in them, but 5 ways of saying the syllable exist.

Through has the (oo) sound.
Bough has the (ow) sound.
Though has the (oh) sound.
Rough has the (uf) sound.
Bought has the (awt) sound.

See why you must be careful in spelling and pronunciation? I cannot tell you why these words are pronounced as such, but you and I can pronounce these with care and study.

<u>Vaseline</u>

Vaseline is a product trademark for a company that makes petroleum jelly. All petroleum jelly products aren't Vaseline. Don't use interchangeably. **See Band-Aid and Kleenex.**

Vulgarity

Avoid vulgarity entirely.

Y'all

The truncated form for *you all* is *y'all.* *You* can be a singular or plural pronoun. Restrict usage to comfortable and informal situations.

You're/Your

Though pronunciation is very similar, these two are spelled differently and have two different meanings. As mentioned earlier, *your* is possessive and *you're* is the contraction for *you are.*

<u>Your, Yours</u>

Never say yorn. There is no "n" in *your* or *yours*. This is another word that many children hear, and then grow up with, without correction. Clean it up now.

> Informal: *Is that mine or yorn?*
> Formal: *Is that mine or yours?*

Chapter 3

The Origin of Black Vernacular English (Black English Dialect)

Before judging or categorizing how people communicate, we must first seek definition. What is Black Vernacular English? Does it even exist? Is it a dialect? Could it possibly be an idiolect or regional dialect? Is it temporal or is it a part of the public dialect? Should it be condemned or used all the time? Answering these questions with one broad theoretical statement would be impossible, but studying the origin of Black Vernacular English as well as why its prevalence remains in the community, becomes the real issue. Imagine being forced to stop speaking your native tongue and suddenly hearing a strange one. What would you do?

Black Vernacular English (from now on it will be referred to as BVE) has an origin that dates back to the year 1619 plus three locations: Africa, the Middle Passage, and America. There is a very interesting bond between these factors and their effects on language. At first glance one might doubt that this phenomenon of speech has any ties to the history and culture of the African-American. Don't be mistaken, because the ties are many.

Slang in the African-American community is widely used. BVE is primarily an effect of slavery, since the common languages from the African continent were dissolved by force. As the languages of Wolof, Swahili, Mandingo and others were sifted out of our mental and verbal familiarity, the English language began to work its way into our psyche. In actuality, a hybrid of language was taking place without Africans and slavemasters alike even realizing it. New words, innovative expressions, fresh ways of phrasing, and unique spellings began inhabiting the English language from an African point of view. The slavemaster wasn't realizing that he was creating a new way of speaking here because of the suppression of culture freedom. Slavemasters were confused because they didn't have a plan of attacking communication amongst "slaves" that was highly effective or suppressive. Many slave holders tried to ban the singing of slaves. Some tried the *bit method* which consisted of placing a large block or bit in the mouth to prevent communication exchange. A popular concept was to prohibit slaves from reading and writing but this was an impractical and far-fetched notion on the master's part. To silence anyone (even through force of violence) is nearly impossible. The voice is the gun and the pen is the sword.

Once this *language restriction-construction* (LRC) began to take root, Africans embarked upon a new way of disseminating (talking) and receiving (hearing) information.1

disseminating (talking) and receiving (hearing) information.1 BVE was born from the cruel institution of slavery, but its devices are still used, held on to, and appreciated by Blacks today because of its effectiveness. Language Restriction-Construction is born from one's restriction to do one thing and one's ability and free will to create another because of the restriction. The construction of BVE was invented from our limited knowledge of the formal English language. We also must attribute this restriction to Europeans who didn't have a formal pattern of speaking and writing English as well. (We mustn't forget that in America, authentic English is not spoken. The English--from England--say that west of the Atlantic, English is not spoken but American is spoken).

Many of the patterns in BVE are still used today and make perfect sense to one who is familiar with the dialect. The problem arises in the broader world or in our case, the United States of America. Everyone in America does not understand BVE. Some Blacks do not speak and understand BVE. Many Europeans do not speak or comprehend BVE. Because the speaking of "so-called" standard American English is important in this society, it is in the best interest of Blacks desiring entrepreneurial, financial, and social mobility to be able to utilize the language of power and finance.2 BVE should not be forgotten, forbiddden, nor forsaken, but there is a time and a place for all activities, speech patterns, attitudes, behaviours, clothing and lifestyles.

Some of the more common African-American expressions that have shown signs of being originated in Africa are the consistent sarcastic teasing remarks (or as we know in this country as playing the dozens). Many west Africans that I've spoken with have related "the dozens" with a form of teasing friends verbally in west Africa. Dr. Geneva Smitherman, a speech and African Studies expert, has studied the languages from Africa and gives two examples of this relationship: the word *hip* which originates from the Wolof language spoken in Senegal and the expressions of opposite such as *bad* meaning *good* (as in: That new Camero she has is *bad.*) 3

African speech characteristics that have been fused into the English language are profound and very useful. When speaking standard American English (SAE), one can lose something in the translation from BVE to SAE. Here's an example. Two ladies are talking about a man who has been unkind to one of the ladies. First the conversation in Black Vernacular English.

What's up girl? Whatchu gon' do wit 'em?
Homegirl, he been illin' from jumpstreet.
Scuse me, girlfriend, whatchu gone do?
Amma drop the zero, next week!
Dats whatchu sed las week.

Now here's the conversation in Standard American English.

> What's going on friend? What are you going to do with him?
> Girlfriend, he hasn't been acting right since the beginning.
>
> Excuse me, friend, so what are you going to do?
> I'm going to break up with that loser next week!
> That's what you told me last week.

The differences between the words, the usage, the accents, and the rhythm are clearly identified here. The message is conveyed in BVE and as you should be able to see, there is a great deal of emphasis lost in the translation to standard English. In the neighborhood, I prefer using BVE because it's comfortable, communicable, colorful, and vast. The importance is in the ability to shift gears into the "other English" when needed.

Shifting gears can be called several things. Some would say that it is *selling out* (assimilation). Others might call verbal gear shifting a form of adaptation or "code switching." It is clear that this skill (the ability to change form BVE to SAE back to BVE) is what one of our more intelligent brothers, W.E.B. DuBois, once alluded to as the *Veil.* The *Veil* is the dual consciousness that inhabits the African-American which he explains in his book, *The Souls of Black Folk.*

> ..the Negro is a sort of seventh son, born with a veil, and gifted with second-sight in this American world, -- a world which yields him no true self-consciousness, but only lets him see himself through the

revelation of the other world. It is a peculiar sensation, this double-consciousness, this sense of always looking at one's self through the eyes of others, of measuring one's soul by the tape of a world that looks on in amused contempt and pity. One ever feels his twoness, -- an American, a Negro; two souls, two thoughts, two unreconciled strivings; two warring ideals in one dark body, whose dogged strength alone keeps it from being torn asunder. **4**

This DuBois quote sums up the African-American experience and its many perplexities and complexities. The question of dialect switching can be equally complex, but great concern should be taken in knowing both and having the knowledge to use them at the *right* times.

Frederick Douglass also teaches us a lesson in his autobiographical essays and letters. Africans were forbidden to learn how to read and he emphatically points out the Black child's need to learn in this poignant quote from his slavemaster.

> If you teach that nigger how to **read**, there would be no keeping him. **Learning** would *spoil* the best nigger in the world. It would forever unfit him to be a slave. If you give a nigger an inch, he will take an ell (45 inches). A nigger should know nothing but to obey his master--to do as he is told to do. **5**

Frederick Douglass goes on to say,

> I now understood what had been to me a most perplexing
> difficulty--to wit, the white man's power to enslave the black
> man (literacy). **6**

If Frederick Douglass said this in 1845 at the age of twenty-eight, what makes us so pompous, headstrong, and arrogant to think that learning the language of power and finance isn't important today? Douglass also states that slavery was perpetuated by the forced illiteracy of Black people.

Chapter 4

The Good and Evil in Rap Music's Language

Rap music is Black America's T.V. station.

Chuck D. [7]

In the world of rap music there are many positive and negative points. This chapter will focus on the perils and triumphs of rap's language. I will have to criticize some rap artists intensely because of their destructive nature. Later in the chapter I will sing praises and give rap its kudos.

Besides many rap artists referring to women as "B's" and "H's" there are many other evils in this industry's warping of the English language. Intentional misspellings on CD and cassette covers, twisted definitions, and mispronunciation in songs all attribute to a new dialect that is fun to listen to and emulate; but if the child is unable to distinguish between the dialect of rap (which is saturated with Black Vernacular English) and the *great midwestern dialect*, you will have a child that will confuse these same concepts in school, church, home, and with his/her friends. It should be obvious why this can be detrimental.

A popular spelling for the word "fat" on many rap CD covers is "phat." It's spelled this way for three reasons: 1) to rebel against traditional English, 2) because it's different (fashionable) and, 3) it is phonetically pronounced the same as "fat." Children (adolescents) are heavily influenced by rap music and it is important for you to teach your child the difference between the standard and non-standard.

The Elements of Style drives this point home even more by listing other more universal examples. Strunk and White state this:

> In ordinary composition, use orthodox spelling. Do not write *nite* for *night*, *thru* for *through*, *pleez* for *please*, unless you plan to introduce a complete system of simplified spelling and are prepared to take the consequences. **8**

Stick to the rules of English to avoid looking inarticulate and unintelligent. Be on the lookout for other terms used in rap that aren't standard. *Three wheel motion, jackin', wack, nine m, gat, skeezer, blowin' up, trues, knobs, knuckles, "G," nigga, rock, Joe, slippin', mack, drop top, low rider, philly, slim, trim, dog, trippin', scope,* and the many other expressions and words that are used in rap can be colorful and comfortable in your environment, but restrict the usage in the situations we've mentioned earlier.

I love rap music and I listen to more rap than anything else (jazz is a close second), but most rap is very degrading to

Black people. Women take major punishment, family morals get thrown out the window, and the respect for the African-American also becomes diminutive. Distinguishing is the key. There is a time and place for rap lingo, but it's not in a formal letter to a corporation. Make sure your child is reading and that the child understands the difference between rap's English and standard American English.

On the other hand, rap is one of the reasons our children have any self-esteem left. It empowers many of our children by saying things that they need to hear. Some rappers choose positive messages such as no sex for unmarried teenagers, staying in school, knowledge of self, self love, and the promotion of reading. Public Enemy, KRS-ONE, Chubb Rock, Paris, and Arrested Development are all champions of positive messages. Just as an Elie Wiesel or Anne Frank would feel obligated to discuss the Holocaust, rap artists feel the obligation to discuss the *middle passage* because they realize "that for four hundred years ships sailed carrying cargo..." [9] Jazz musician, Donald Byrd, defends Rap music by making this statement,

Rap music is a poetic form criticized because
many who criticize it cannot do it successfully. [10]

Rap groups like Public Enemy, Ice Cube, and Paris are looked upon as being more pugnacious and militant in their approach, however their lyrics state the truth about Black Americans and how Black people feel. Arrested Development and others are considered more gentle in lyrical content but they also manage to instill responsible behaviour in their CDs from treating women right to becoming a productive citizen in society. Rap music is a medium that influences heavily on our children and we must monitor (not censor) the lyrics they're taking in consciously and subconsciously.

For your child, show the distinction between what's right and wrong lyrically. Some rappers stretch the truth through exaggeration to reinforce a point. As long as the child realizes that the rap artist is an *artist* (entertainer) he or she should be able to not take the rapper literally all of the time. This is the parents' responsibility even though the parent may not get to listen to all of the rap music in the child's collection.

Rap's strongest ally is the music (beat, bass line, and samples). Many times lyrics aren't understandable because of the music drowning or the regional dialect. But most lyrics are easily heard and can be offensive. Beware!

Chapter 5

Black Leaders Use Standard English

Our most powerful Black leaders speak and have spoken standard American English better than many other intellectuals, regardless of race. The diction of Malcolm X was nearly flawless and Malcolm did this on his own volition (reading various books including the dictionary while in prison). Malcolm realized that the best way to impart knowledge was to simply communicate through standard American English. Listen to some of Malcolm's speeches and watch X on video tape. His articulation and precision will make your skin crawl.

Barbara Jordan's command of the English language has taken her to the top. As a convention keynote speaker, she has made women as well as African-Americans proud of the strides that have been accomplished.

Maya Angelou's poems and Terry McMillan's stories have touched many of us dearly. These two ladies capture the essence of our culture and history in their works.

W.E.B. DuBois, James Baldwin, Richard Wright, Dr. Carter G. Woodson, and Ralph Ellison have shown us the social and psychological problems that have plagued the African-American with their exemplary writing.

Dr. Martin Luther King, Jr., was also one with epitomizing enunciation and verbal expression. King's words sounded like music and his metaphors and similes were far better than many great poets that I have read. Why would a person not want to intonate like these men and women? These are definitely good role models.

Even superstar musicians, entertainers, and athletes find it in their best interest to command the language with consistency. Good diction promotes more interviews and exposure. Michael Jordan is a classic example of a brother who speaks well. I love to hear him talk about the game of basketball because he talks about the science of the game as well as the fun involved. Wouldn't it be embarrassing if the greatest player in the NBA could not speak standard American English? When someone goes to the microphone or podium to speak, haven't we all felt that nervous tension? I don't like that feeling. I'm proud of Mike because of his playing and speaking abilities. Kevin Johnson, David Robinson, Patrick Ewing, Charles Barkley, Charles Oakley, Scottie Pippen, and others also use the language well and consequently end up with the most *playing time* on the microphone during interviews.

We must start realizing in the words of Jesse Jackson that *excellence transcends race*. Speaking standard American English isn't *selling out*, or being a *Tom*. Using your best diction will enable you to get ahead in the United States. Oprah Winfrey, Ahmad Rashad, Bill Cosby, Greg and Bryant

Gumble, John Rogers, and Jawanza Kunjufu wouldn't be where they are if they exercised poor communication skills. We as a people have to take the road that will lead us to the promised land: the land of milk and honey, the road that leads to our success as a people.

The average African-American child wants *success*. What we as adults have to do is to identify what success is and to show our children what steps and measures have to be taken to achieve this goal. Use of language is one of those measures. There is nothing wrong with a child wanting to be a professional basketball player but the odds are too great to take that chance alone (only 6 out of 2 million Division 1 NCAA athletes make it into the pros).

Let's teach our children and educate our adults about the pitfalls we all suffer in this war against illiteracy. Standard American English isn't a difficult thing to master but it takes time, patience, an open mind, and a big piece of humble pie. Study the examples in this book and also see Dr. Evelyn B. Dandy's book entitled, *Black Communications: Breaking Down the Barriers* (African-American Images Publishing).

Author's Closing Comments

Study English with intensity. Read an entire book every ten days. Try to pick up a newspaper daily along with a news magazine once per week. Limit television viewing. Research things you know and don't know. Go to libraries often. Attend lectures and take notes with paper, pen, and tape recorder. Be able to command the English language.

With the love of Christ,

Garrard McClendon

NOTES

1. Garrard McClendon. *Slavery and Speech*. Hammond: Positive People Publishing, 1992, p. 1.

2. Excerpt from a quoted sound bite from Bernadette Anderson on the *Oprah Winfrey Show--Black English*. WLS-TV Chicago: Harpo Productions, 1989.

3. Ibid., Dr. Geneva Smitherman.

4. W.E.B. DuBois. *The Souls of Black Folk*. New York: A Signet Classic, 1903, p. 45.

5. Frederick Douglass. *The Classic Slave Narratives: Narrative of the Life of Frederick Douglass.* (written circa 1845). New York: Penguin/Mentor, 1987, p.274.

6. Ibid., p.275.

7. Excerpt from a quoted sound bite from Chuck D. (from the rap group *Public Enemy*) on Black Entertainment Television. Washington, D.C: BET, 1990.

8. Strunk and White *The Elements of Style,* New York: Macmillan, 1959, p. 74.

9. Hank Shocklee. Chuck D., from Public Enemy song, *Can't "Truss" It.*, 1991.

10. Donald Byrd quoted by Dr. John Alston (English Professor:Wabash College), 1989.

BIBLIOGRAPHY

Voices of Struggle/Voices of Pride (Beilenson and Jackson)
Black English (Dillard)
Handbook of Current English (Corder and Ruszkiewicz)
Notes of a Hanging Judge (Crouch)
The Souls of Black Folk (DuBois)
The Classic Slave Narratives (Edited by H.L. Gates)
Countering the Conspiracy to Destroy Black Boys (Kunjufu)
To Be Popular or Smart (Kunjufu)
Developing Positive Self-Images in Black Children (Kunjufu)
Malcolm X Talks to Young People (Malcolm X)
Malcolm X on Afro-American History (Malcolm X)
The Elements of Style (William Strunk and E.B. White)
The Little Black Book (Taylor)
The Mis-Education of the Negro (Woodson)
Heath Grammar and Composition
Webster's Handy College Dictionary
The Pocket Oxford Dictionary
The Random House Dictionary of the English Language
(Second Edition -- Unabridged)

Solitude

All writers need to be alone to think, create, and produce their work. Writing in a big city is distracting for me and I must express my appreciation for the city of Culver, IN, and the Culver Academies.

Teaching here has been a joy and I thank Ralph Manuel and Alexander Nagy for the opportunity to share my teaching skills at such a prestigious academy.

Paul Hamer has been an inspiration. As my supervisor, he has been a great model as a writer, teacher, and thinker. Thank you for supporting my teaching style, encouraging the speech team, and pushing me toward the masters degree.

The original manuscript was written at the Culver Academies with special courtesy from the Educational Technology Department. The Apple Powerbook was my best friend for the 7 month writing binge and I want to thank Chris Clark, Pat Renneker, and Bruce Holaday for putting up with me and answering all of my tedious Macintosh questions.

Average S.A.T. Verbal Scores
According to Ethnicity

White (European-Americans)	444
Asian-Americans	415
American Indian	400
Mexican-American	374
Puerto Rican	367
Black (African-Americans)	**353**

*Education Week   September 1993

Notes

The African-American Guide
To Better English

Notes

The African-American Guide
To Better English